This notebook contains important information.

If you return it to it's rightful owner, you'll get a big sloppy kiss on the face from an overweight Chocolate Labrador Retriever.

If you don't return it, you'll slip on a banana today, it's up to you.

Return to:_____

Phone:_____

Email:_____

Date: _____

Lesson start time:_____ End time:_____

Client name:_____

Dog name:_____

Phone number :_____

Additional information about the client or dog to remember?_____

_____

Does the dog have any health issues or food allergies? (Y) (N)

Does the dog have a history of aggression? (Y) (N)

Where did you do the lesson?_____

Which lesson is this?_____

What did you work on during this lesson?_____

_____

_____

Homework given to your client:_____

_____

_____

_____

Additional notes:_____

_____

_____

_____

Next Lesson:_____

Date: _____

Lesson start time:_____ End time:_____

Client name:_____

Dog name:_____

Phone number :_____

Additional information about the client or dog to remember?_____

_____

Does the dog have any health issues or food allergies? (Y) (N)

Does the dog have a history of aggression? (Y) (N)

Where did you do the lesson?_____

Which lesson is this?_____

What did you work on during this lesson?_____

_____

_____

Homework given to your client:_____

_____

_____

_____

Additional notes:_____

_____

_____

_____

Next Lesson:_____

Date: _____

Lesson start time:_____ End time:_____

Client name:_____

Dog name:_____

Phone number :_____

Additional information about the client or dog to remember?_____

_____

Does the dog have any health issues or food allergies? (Y) (N)

Does the dog have a history of aggression? (Y) (N)

Where did you do the lesson?_____

Which lesson is this?_____

What did you work on during this lesson?_____

_____

_____

Homework given to your client:_____

_____

_____

_____

Additional notes:_____

_____

_____

_____

Next Lesson:_____

Date: _____

Lesson start time:_____ End time:_____

Client name:_____

Dog name:_____

Phone number :_____

Additional information about the client or dog to remember?_____

_____

Does the dog have any health issues or food allergies? (Y) (N)

Does the dog have a history of aggression? (Y) (N)

Where did you do the lesson?_____

Which lesson is this?_____

What did you work on during this lesson?_____

_____

_____

Homework given to your client:_____

_____

_____

_____

Additional notes:_____

_____

_____

_____

Next Lesson:_____

Date: _____

Lesson start time:_____ End time:_____

Client name:_____

Dog name:_____

Phone number :_____

Additional information about the client or dog to remember?_____

_____

Does the dog have any health issues or food allergies? (Y) (N)

Does the dog have a history of aggression? (Y) (N)

Where did you do the lesson?_____

Which lesson is this?_____

What did you work on during this lesson?_____

_____

_____

Homework given to your client:_____

_____

_____

_____

Additional notes:_____

_____

_____

_____

Next Lesson:_____

Date: _____

Lesson start time:_____ End time:_____

Client name:_____

Dog name:_____

Phone number :_____

Additional information about the client or dog to remember?_____

_____

Does the dog have any health issues or food allergies? (Y) (N)

Does the dog have a history of aggression? (Y) (N)

Where did you do the lesson?_____

Which lesson is this?_____

What did you work on during this lesson?_____

_____

_____

Homework given to your client:_____

_____

_____

_____

Additional notes:_____

_____

_____

_____

Next Lesson:_____

Date: _____

Lesson start time:_____ End time:_____

Client name:_____

Dog name:_____

Phone number :_____

Additional information about the client or dog to remember?_____

_____

Does the dog have any health issues or food allergies? (Y) (N)

Does the dog have a history of aggression? (Y) (N)

Where did you do the lesson?_____

Which lesson is this?_____

What did you work on during this lesson?_____

_____

_____

Homework given to your client:_____

_____

_____

_____

Additional notes:_____

_____

_____

_____

Next Lesson:_____

Date: _____

Lesson start time:_____ End time:_____

Client name:_____

Dog name:_____

Phone number :_____

Additional information about the client or dog to remember?_____

_____

Does the dog have any health issues or food allergies? (Y) (N)

Does the dog have a history of aggression? (Y) (N)

Where did you do the lesson?_____

Which lesson is this?_____

What did you work on during this lesson?_____

_____

_____

Homework given to your client:_____

_____

_____

_____

Additional notes:_____

_____

_____

_____

Next Lesson:_____

Date: _____

Lesson start time:_____ End time:_____

Client name:_____

Dog name:_____

Phone number :_____

Additional information about the client or dog to remember?_____

_____

Does the dog have any health issues or food allergies? (Y) (N)

Does the dog have a history of aggression? (Y) (N)

Where did you do the lesson?_____

Which lesson is this?_____

What did you work on during this lesson?_____

_____

_____

Homework given to your client:_____

_____

_____

_____

Additional notes:_____

_____

_____

_____

Next Lesson:_____

Date: _____

Lesson start time:_____ End time:_____

Client name:_____

Dog name:_____

Phone number :_____

Additional information about the client or dog to remember?_____

_____

Does the dog have any health issues or food allergies? (Y) (N)

Does the dog have a history of aggression? (Y) (N)

Where did you do the lesson?_____

Which lesson is this?_____

What did you work on during this lesson?_____

_____

_____

Homework given to your client:_____

_____

_____

_____

Additional notes:_____

_____

_____

_____

Next Lesson:_____

Date: _____

Lesson start time:_____ End time:_____

Client name:_____

Dog name:_____

Phone number :_____

Additional information about the client or dog to remember?_____

_____

Does the dog have any health issues or food allergies? (Y) (N)

Does the dog have a history of aggression? (Y) (N)

Where did you do the lesson?_____

Which lesson is this?_____

What did you work on during this lesson?_____

_____

_____

Homework given to your client:_____

_____

_____

_____

Additional notes:_____

_____

_____

_____

Next Lesson:_____

Date: _____

Lesson start time:_____ End time:_____

Client name:_____

Dog name:_____

Phone number :_____

Additional information about the client or dog to remember?_____

_____

Does the dog have any health issues or food allergies? (Y) (N)

Does the dog have a history of aggression? (Y) (N)

Where did you do the lesson?_____

Which lesson is this?_____

What did you work on during this lesson?_____

_____

_____

Homework given to your client:_____

_____

_____

_____

Additional notes:_____

_____

_____

_____

Next Lesson:_____

Date: _____

Lesson start time:_____ End time:_____

Client name:_____

Dog name:_____

Phone number :_____

Additional information about the client or dog to remember?_____

_____

Does the dog have any health issues or food allergies? (Y) (N)

Does the dog have a history of aggression? (Y) (N)

Where did you do the lesson?_____

Which lesson is this?_____

What did you work on during this lesson?_____

_____

_____

Homework given to your client:_____

_____

_____

_____

Additional notes:_____

_____

_____

_____

Next Lesson:_____

Date: _____

Lesson start time:_____ End time:_____

Client name:_____

Dog name:_____

Phone number :_____

Additional information about the client or dog to remember?_____

_____

Does the dog have any health issues or food allergies? (Y) (N)

Does the dog have a history of aggression? (Y) (N)

Where did you do the lesson?_____

Which lesson is this?_____

What did you work on during this lesson?_____

_____

_____

Homework given to your client:_____

_____

_____

_____

Additional notes:_____

_____

_____

_____

Next Lesson:_____

Date: _____

Lesson start time:_____ End time:_____

Client name:_____

Dog name:_____

Phone number :_____

Additional information about the client or dog to remember?_____

_____

Does the dog have any health issues or food allergies? (Y) (N)

Does the dog have a history of aggression? (Y) (N)

Where did you do the lesson?_____

Which lesson is this?_____

What did you work on during this lesson?_____

_____

_____

Homework given to your client:_____

_____

_____

_____

Additional notes:_____

_____

_____

_____

Next Lesson:_____

Date: _____

Lesson start time:_____ End time:_____

Client name:_____

Dog name:_____

Phone number :_____

Additional information about the client or dog to remember?_____

_____

Does the dog have any health issues or food allergies? (Y) (N)

Does the dog have a history of aggression? (Y) (N)

Where did you do the lesson?_____

Which lesson is this?_____

What did you work on during this lesson?_____

_____

_____

Homework given to your client:_____

_____

_____

_____

Additional notes:_____

_____

_____

_____

Next Lesson:_____

Date: _____

Lesson start time:_____ End time:_____

Client name:_____

Dog name:_____

Phone number :_____

Additional information about the client or dog to remember?_____

_____

Does the dog have any health issues or food allergies? (Y) (N)

Does the dog have a history of aggression? (Y) (N)

Where did you do the lesson?_____

Which lesson is this?_____

What did you work on during this lesson?_____

_____

_____

Homework given to your client:_____

_____

_____

_____

Additional notes:_____

_____

_____

_____

Next Lesson:_____

Date: _____

Lesson start time:_____ End time:_____

Client name:_____

Dog name:_____

Phone number :_____

Additional information about the client or dog to remember?_____

_____

Does the dog have any health issues or food allergies? (Y) (N)

Does the dog have a history of aggression? (Y) (N)

Where did you do the lesson?_____

Which lesson is this?_____

What did you work on during this lesson?_____

_____

_____

Homework given to your client:_____

_____

_____

_____

Additional notes:_____

_____

_____

_____

Next Lesson:_____

Date: _____

Lesson start time:_____ End time:_____

Client name:_____

Dog name:_____

Phone number :_____

Additional information about the client or dog to remember?_____

_____

Does the dog have any health issues or food allergies? (Y) (N)

Does the dog have a history of aggression? (Y) (N)

Where did you do the lesson?_____

Which lesson is this?_____

What did you work on during this lesson?_____

_____

_____

Homework given to your client:_____

_____

_____

_____

Additional notes:_____

_____

_____

_____

Next Lesson:_____

Date: _____

Lesson start time:_____ End time:_____

Client name:_____

Dog name:_____

Phone number :_____

Additional information about the client or dog to remember?_____

_____

Does the dog have any health issues or food allergies? (Y) (N)

Does the dog have a history of aggression? (Y) (N)

Where did you do the lesson?_____

Which lesson is this?_____

What did you work on during this lesson?_____

_____

_____

Homework given to your client:_____

_____

_____

_____

Additional notes:_____

_____

_____

_____

Next Lesson:_____

Date: _____

Lesson start time:_____ End time:_____

Client name:_____

Dog name:_____

Phone number :_____

Additional information about the client or dog to remember?_____

_____

Does the dog have any health issues or food allergies? (Y) (N)

Does the dog have a history of aggression? (Y) (N)

Where did you do the lesson?_____

Which lesson is this?_____

What did you work on during this lesson?_____

_____

_____

Homework given to your client:_____

_____

_____

_____

Additional notes:_____

_____

_____

_____

Next Lesson:_____

Date: _____

Lesson start time:_____ End time:_____

Client name:_____

Dog name:_____

Phone number :_____

Additional information about the client or dog to remember?_____

_____

Does the dog have any health issues or food allergies? (Y) (N)

Does the dog have a history of aggression? (Y) (N)

Where did you do the lesson?_____

Which lesson is this?_____

What did you work on during this lesson?_____

_____

_____

Homework given to your client:_____

_____

_____

_____

Additional notes:_____

_____

_____

_____

Next Lesson:_____

Date: _____

Lesson start time:_____ End time:_____

Client name:_____

Dog name:_____

Phone number :_____

Additional information about the client or dog to remember?_____

_____

Does the dog have any health issues or food allergies? (Y) (N)

Does the dog have a history of aggression? (Y) (N)

Where did you do the lesson?_____

Which lesson is this?_____

What did you work on during this lesson?_____

_____

_____

Homework given to your client:_____

_____

_____

_____

Additional notes:_____

_____

_____

_____

Next Lesson:_____

Date: _____

Lesson start time:_____ End time:_____

Client name:_____

Dog name:_____

Phone number :_____

Additional information about the client or dog to remember?_____

_____

Does the dog have any health issues or food allergies? (Y) (N)

Does the dog have a history of aggression? (Y) (N)

Where did you do the lesson?_____

Which lesson is this?_____

What did you work on during this lesson?_____

_____

_____

Homework given to your client:_____

_____

_____

_____

Additional notes:_____

_____

_____

_____

Next Lesson:_____

Date: _____

Lesson start time:_____ End time:_____

Client name:_____

Dog name:_____

Phone number :_____

Additional information about the client or dog to remember?_____

_____

Does the dog have any health issues or food allergies? (Y) (N)

Does the dog have a history of aggression? (Y) (N)

Where did you do the lesson?_____

Which lesson is this?_____

What did you work on during this lesson?_____

_____

_____

Homework given to your client:_____

_____

_____

_____

Additional notes:_____

_____

_____

_____

Next Lesson:_____

Date: _____

Lesson start time:_____ End time:_____

Client name:_____

Dog name:_____

Phone number :_____

Additional information about the client or dog to remember?_____

_____

Does the dog have any health issues or food allergies? (Y) (N)

Does the dog have a history of aggression? (Y) (N)

Where did you do the lesson?_____

Which lesson is this?_____

What did you work on during this lesson?_____

_____

_____

Homework given to your client:_____

_____

_____

_____

Additional notes:_____

_____

_____

_____

Next Lesson:_____

Date: _____

Lesson start time:_____ End time:_____

Client name:_____

Dog name:_____

Phone number :_____

Additional information about the client or dog to remember?_____

_____

Does the dog have any health issues or food allergies? (Y) (N)

Does the dog have a history of aggression? (Y) (N)

Where did you do the lesson?_____

Which lesson is this?_____

What did you work on during this lesson?_____

_____

_____

Homework given to your client:_____

_____

_____

_____

Additional notes:_____

_____

_____

_____

Next Lesson:_____

Date: _____

Lesson start time:_____ End time:_____

Client name:_____

Dog name:_____

Phone number :_____

Additional information about the client or dog to remember?_____

_____

Does the dog have any health issues or food allergies? (Y) (N)

Does the dog have a history of aggression? (Y) (N)

Where did you do the lesson?_____

Which lesson is this?_____

What did you work on during this lesson?_____

_____

_____

Homework given to your client:_____

_____

_____

_____

Additional notes:_____

_____

_____

_____

Next Lesson:_____

Date: _____

Lesson start time:_____ End time:_____

Client name:_____

Dog name:_____

Phone number :_____

Additional information about the client or dog to remember?_____

_____

Does the dog have any health issues or food allergies? (Y) (N)

Does the dog have a history of aggression? (Y) (N)

Where did you do the lesson?_____

Which lesson is this?_____

What did you work on during this lesson?_____

_____

_____

Homework given to your client:_____

_____

_____

_____

Additional notes:_____

_____

_____

_____

Next Lesson:_____

Date: _____

Lesson start time:_____ End time:_____

Client name:_____

Dog name:_____

Phone number :_____

Additional information about the client or dog to remember?_____

_____

Does the dog have any health issues or food allergies? (Y) (N)

Does the dog have a history of aggression? (Y) (N)

Where did you do the lesson?_____

Which lesson is this?_____

What did you work on during this lesson?_____

_____

_____

Homework given to your client:_____

_____

_____

_____

Additional notes:_____

_____

_____

_____

Next Lesson:_____

Date: _____

Lesson start time:_____ End time:_____

Client name:_____

Dog name:_____

Phone number :_____

Additional information about the client or dog to remember?_____

_____

Does the dog have any health issues or food allergies? (Y) (N)

Does the dog have a history of aggression? (Y) (N)

Where did you do the lesson?_____

Which lesson is this?_____

What did you work on during this lesson?_____

_____

_____

Homework given to your client:_____

_____

_____

_____

Additional notes:_____

_____

_____

_____

Next Lesson:_____

Date: _____

Lesson start time:_____ End time:_____

Client name:_____

Dog name:_____

Phone number :_____

Additional information about the client or dog to remember?_____

_____

Does the dog have any health issues or food allergies? (Y) (N)

Does the dog have a history of aggression? (Y) (N)

Where did you do the lesson?_____

Which lesson is this?_____

What did you work on during this lesson?_____

_____

_____

Homework given to your client:_____

_____

_____

_____

Additional notes:_____

_____

_____

_____

Next Lesson:_____

Date: _____

Lesson start time:_____ End time:_____

Client name:_____

Dog name:_____

Phone number :_____

Additional information about the client or dog to remember?_____

_____

Does the dog have any health issues or food allergies? (Y) (N)

Does the dog have a history of aggression? (Y) (N)

Where did you do the lesson?_____

Which lesson is this?_____

What did you work on during this lesson?_____

_____

_____

Homework given to your client:_____

_____

_____

_____

Additional notes:_____

_____

_____

_____

Next Lesson:_____

Date: _____

Lesson start time:_____ End time:_____

Client name:_____

Dog name:_____

Phone number :_____

Additional information about the client or dog to remember?_____

_____

Does the dog have any health issues or food allergies? (Y) (N)

Does the dog have a history of aggression? (Y) (N)

Where did you do the lesson?_____

Which lesson is this?_____

What did you work on during this lesson?_____

_____

_____

Homework given to your client:_____

_____

_____

_____

Additional notes:_____

_____

_____

_____

Next Lesson:_____

Date: _____

Lesson start time:_____ End time:_____

Client name:_____

Dog name:_____

Phone number :_____

Additional information about the client or dog to remember?_____

_____

Does the dog have any health issues or food allergies? (Y) (N)

Does the dog have a history of aggression? (Y) (N)

Where did you do the lesson?_____

Which lesson is this?_____

What did you work on during this lesson?_____

_____

_____

Homework given to your client:_____

_____

_____

_____

Additional notes:_____

_____

_____

_____

Next Lesson:_____

Date: _____

Lesson start time:_____ End time:_____

Client name:_____

Dog name:_____

Phone number :_____

Additional information about the client or dog to remember?_____

_____

Does the dog have any health issues or food allergies? (Y) (N)

Does the dog have a history of aggression? (Y) (N)

Where did you do the lesson?_____

Which lesson is this?_____

What did you work on during this lesson?_____

_____

_____

Homework given to your client:_____

_____

_____

_____

Additional notes:_____

_____

_____

_____

Next Lesson:_____

Date: _____

Lesson start time:_____ End time:_____

Client name:_____

Dog name:_____

Phone number :_____

Additional information about the client or dog to remember?_____

_____

Does the dog have any health issues or food allergies? (Y) (N)

Does the dog have a history of aggression? (Y) (N)

Where did you do the lesson?_____

Which lesson is this?_____

What did you work on during this lesson?_____

_____

_____

Homework given to your client:_____

_____

_____

_____

Additional notes:_____

_____

_____

_____

Next Lesson:_____

Date: _____

Lesson start time:_____ End time:_____

Client name:_____

Dog name:_____

Phone number :_____

Additional information about the client or dog to remember?_____

_____

Does the dog have any health issues or food allergies? (Y) (N)

Does the dog have a history of aggression? (Y) (N)

Where did you do the lesson?_____

Which lesson is this?_____

What did you work on during this lesson?_____

_____

_____

Homework given to your client:_____

_____

_____

_____

Additional notes:_____

_____

_____

_____

Next Lesson:_____

Date: _____

Lesson start time:_____ End time:_____

Client name:_____

Dog name:_____

Phone number :_____

Additional information about the client or dog to remember?_____

_____

Does the dog have any health issues or food allergies? (Y) (N)

Does the dog have a history of aggression? (Y) (N)

Where did you do the lesson?_____

Which lesson is this?_____

What did you work on during this lesson?_____

_____

_____

Homework given to your client:_____

_____

_____

_____

Additional notes:_____

_____

_____

_____

Next Lesson:_____

Date: _____

Lesson start time:_____ End time:_____

Client name:_____

Dog name:_____

Phone number :_____

Additional information about the client or dog to remember?_____

_____

Does the dog have any health issues or food allergies? (Y) (N)

Does the dog have a history of aggression? (Y) (N)

Where did you do the lesson?_____

Which lesson is this?_____

What did you work on during this lesson?_____

_____

_____

Homework given to your client:_____

_____

_____

_____

Additional notes:_____

_____

_____

_____

Next Lesson:_____

Date: _____

Lesson start time:_____ End time:_____

Client name:_____

Dog name:_____

Phone number :_____

Additional information about the client or dog to remember?_____

_____

Does the dog have any health issues or food allergies? (Y) (N)

Does the dog have a history of aggression? (Y) (N)

Where did you do the lesson?_____

Which lesson is this?_____

What did you work on during this lesson?_____

_____

_____

Homework given to your client:_____

_____

_____

_____

Additional notes:_____

_____

_____

_____

Next Lesson:_____

Date: _____

Lesson start time:_____ End time:_____

Client name:_____

Dog name:_____

Phone number :_____

Additional information about the client or dog to remember?_____

_____

Does the dog have any health issues or food allergies? (Y) (N)

Does the dog have a history of aggression? (Y) (N)

Where did you do the lesson?_____

Which lesson is this?_____

What did you work on during this lesson?_____

_____

_____

Homework given to your client:_____

_____

_____

_____

Additional notes:_____

_____

_____

_____

Next Lesson:_____

Date: _____

Lesson start time:_____ End time:_____

Client name:_____

Dog name:_____

Phone number :_____

Additional information about the client or dog to remember?_____

_____

Does the dog have any health issues or food allergies? (Y) (N)

Does the dog have a history of aggression? (Y) (N)

Where did you do the lesson?_____

Which lesson is this?_____

What did you work on during this lesson?_____

_____

_____

Homework given to your client:_____

_____

_____

_____

Additional notes:_____

_____

_____

_____

Next Lesson:_____

Date: _____

Lesson start time:_____ End time:_____

Client name:_____

Dog name:_____

Phone number :_____

Additional information about the client or dog to remember?_____

_____

Does the dog have any health issues or food allergies? (Y) (N)

Does the dog have a history of aggression? (Y) (N)

Where did you do the lesson?_____

Which lesson is this?_____

What did you work on during this lesson?_____

_____

_____

Homework given to your client:_____

_____

_____

_____

Additional notes:_____

_____

_____

_____

Next Lesson:_____

Date: _____

Lesson start time:_____ End time:_____

Client name:_____

Dog name:_____

Phone number :_____

Additional information about the client or dog to remember?_____

_____

Does the dog have any health issues or food allergies? (Y) (N)

Does the dog have a history of aggression? (Y) (N)

Where did you do the lesson?_____

Which lesson is this?_____

What did you work on during this lesson?_____

_____

_____

Homework given to your client:_____

_____

_____

_____

Additional notes:_____

_____

_____

_____

Next Lesson:_____

Date: _____

Lesson start time:_____ End time:_____

Client name:_____

Dog name:_____

Phone number :_____

Additional information about the client or dog to remember?_____

_____

Does the dog have any health issues or food allergies? (Y) (N)

Does the dog have a history of aggression? (Y) (N)

Where did you do the lesson?_____

Which lesson is this?_____

What did you work on during this lesson?_____

_____

_____

Homework given to your client:_____

_____

_____

_____

Additional notes:_____

_____

_____

_____

Next Lesson:_____

Date: _____

Lesson start time:_____ End time:_____

Client name:_____

Dog name:_____

Phone number :_____

Additional information about the client or dog to remember?_____

_____

Does the dog have any health issues or food allergies? (Y) (N)

Does the dog have a history of aggression? (Y) (N)

Where did you do the lesson?_____

Which lesson is this?_____

What did you work on during this lesson?_____

_____

_____

Homework given to your client:_____

_____

_____

_____

Additional notes:_____

_____

_____

_____

Next Lesson:_____

Date: _____

Lesson start time:_____ End time:_____

Client name:_____

Dog name:_____

Phone number :_____

Additional information about the client or dog to remember?_____

_____

Does the dog have any health issues or food allergies? (Y) (N)

Does the dog have a history of aggression? (Y) (N)

Where did you do the lesson?_____

Which lesson is this?_____

What did you work on during this lesson?_____

_____

_____

Homework given to your client:_____

_____

_____

_____

Additional notes:_____

_____

_____

_____

Next Lesson:_____

Date: _____

Lesson start time:_____ End time:_____

Client name:_____

Dog name:_____

Phone number :_____

Additional information about the client or dog to remember?_____

_____

Does the dog have any health issues or food allergies? (Y) (N)

Does the dog have a history of aggression? (Y) (N)

Where did you do the lesson?_____

Which lesson is this?_____

What did you work on during this lesson?_____

_____

_____

Homework given to your client:_____

_____

_____

_____

Additional notes:_____

_____

_____

_____

Next Lesson:_____

Date: _____

Lesson start time:_____ End time:_____

Client name:_____

Dog name:_____

Phone number :_____

Additional information about the client or dog to remember?_____

_____

Does the dog have any health issues or food allergies? (Y) (N)

Does the dog have a history of aggression? (Y) (N)

Where did you do the lesson?_____

Which lesson is this?_____

What did you work on during this lesson?_____

_____

_____

Homework given to your client:_____

_____

_____

_____

Additional notes:_____

_____

_____

_____

Next Lesson:_____

Date: _____

Lesson start time:_____ End time:_____

Client name:_____

Dog name:_____

Phone number :_____

Additional information about the client or dog to remember?_____

_____

Does the dog have any health issues or food allergies? (Y) (N)

Does the dog have a history of aggression? (Y) (N)

Where did you do the lesson?_____

Which lesson is this?_____

What did you work on during this lesson?_____

_____

_____

Homework given to your client:_____

_____

_____

_____

Additional notes:_____

_____

_____

_____

Next Lesson:_____

Date: _____

Lesson start time:_____ End time:_____

Client name:_____

Dog name:_____

Phone number :_____

Additional information about the client or dog to remember?_____

_____

Does the dog have any health issues or food allergies? (Y) (N)

Does the dog have a history of aggression? (Y) (N)

Where did you do the lesson?_____

Which lesson is this?_____

What did you work on during this lesson?_____

_____

_____

Homework given to your client:_____

_____

_____

_____

Additional notes:_____

_____

_____

_____

Next Lesson:_____

Date: _____

Lesson start time:_____ End time:_____

Client name:_____

Dog name:_____

Phone number :_____

Additional information about the client or dog to remember?_____

_____

Does the dog have any health issues or food allergies? (Y) (N)

Does the dog have a history of aggression? (Y) (N)

Where did you do the lesson?_____

Which lesson is this?_____

What did you work on during this lesson?_____

_____

_____

Homework given to your client:_____

_____

_____

_____

Additional notes:_____

_____

_____

_____

Next Lesson:_____

Date: _____

Lesson start time:_____ End time:_____

Client name:_____

Dog name:_____

Phone number :_____

Additional information about the client or dog to remember?_____

_____

Does the dog have any health issues or food allergies? (Y) (N)

Does the dog have a history of aggression? (Y) (N)

Where did you do the lesson?_____

Which lesson is this?_____

What did you work on during this lesson?_____

_____

_____

Homework given to your client:_____

_____

_____

_____

Additional notes:_____

_____

_____

_____

Next Lesson:_____

Date: _____

Lesson start time:_____ End time:_____

Client name:_____

Dog name:_____

Phone number :_____

Additional information about the client or dog to remember?_____

_____

Does the dog have any health issues or food allergies? (Y) (N)

Does the dog have a history of aggression? (Y) (N)

Where did you do the lesson?_____

Which lesson is this?_____

What did you work on during this lesson?_____

_____

_____

Homework given to your client:_____

_____

_____

_____

Additional notes:_____

_____

_____

_____

Next Lesson:_____

Date: _____

Lesson start time:_____ End time:_____

Client name:_____

Dog name:_____

Phone number :_____

Additional information about the client or dog to remember?_____

_____

Does the dog have any health issues or food allergies? (Y) (N)

Does the dog have a history of aggression? (Y) (N)

Where did you do the lesson?_____

Which lesson is this?_____

What did you work on during this lesson?_____

_____

_____

Homework given to your client:_____

_____

_____

_____

Additional notes:_____

_____

_____

_____

Next Lesson:_____

Date: _____

Lesson start time:_____ End time:_____

Client name:_____

Dog name:_____

Phone number :_____

Additional information about the client or dog to remember?_____

_____

Does the dog have any health issues or food allergies? (Y) (N)

Does the dog have a history of aggression? (Y) (N)

Where did you do the lesson?_____

Which lesson is this?_____

What did you work on during this lesson?_____

_____

_____

Homework given to your client:_____

_____

_____

_____

Additional notes:_____

_____

_____

_____

Next Lesson:_____

Date: _____

Lesson start time:_____ End time:_____

Client name:_____

Dog name:_____

Phone number :_____

Additional information about the client or dog to remember?_____

_____

Does the dog have any health issues or food allergies? (Y) (N)

Does the dog have a history of aggression? (Y) (N)

Where did you do the lesson?_____

Which lesson is this?_____

What did you work on during this lesson?_____

_____

_____

Homework given to your client:_____

_____

_____

_____

Additional notes:_____

_____

_____

_____

Next Lesson:_____

Date: _____

Lesson start time:_____ End time:_____

Client name:_____

Dog name:_____

Phone number :_____

Additional information about the client or dog to remember?_____

_____

Does the dog have any health issues or food allergies? (Y) (N)

Does the dog have a history of aggression? (Y) (N)

Where did you do the lesson?_____

Which lesson is this?_____

What did you work on during this lesson?_____

_____

_____

Homework given to your client:_____

_____

_____

_____

Additional notes:_____

_____

_____

_____

Next Lesson:_____

Date: _____

Lesson start time:_____ End time:_____

Client name:_____

Dog name:_____

Phone number :_____

Additional information about the client or dog to remember?_____

_____

Does the dog have any health issues or food allergies? (Y) (N)

Does the dog have a history of aggression? (Y) (N)

Where did you do the lesson?_____

Which lesson is this?_____

What did you work on during this lesson?_____

_____

_____

Homework given to your client:_____

_____

_____

_____

Additional notes:_____

_____

_____

_____

Next Lesson:_____

Date: _____

Lesson start time:_____ End time:_____

Client name:_____

Dog name:_____

Phone number :_____

Additional information about the client or dog to remember?_____

_____

Does the dog have any health issues or food allergies? (Y) (N)

Does the dog have a history of aggression? (Y) (N)

Where did you do the lesson?_____

Which lesson is this?_____

What did you work on during this lesson?_____

_____

_____

Homework given to your client:_____

_____

_____

_____

Additional notes:_____

_____

_____

_____

Next Lesson:_____

Date: _____

Lesson start time:_____ End time:_____

Client name:_____

Dog name:_____

Phone number :_____

Additional information about the client or dog to remember?_____

_____

Does the dog have any health issues or food allergies? (Y) (N)

Does the dog have a history of aggression? (Y) (N)

Where did you do the lesson?_____

Which lesson is this?_____

What did you work on during this lesson?_____

_____

_____

Homework given to your client:_____

_____

_____

_____

Additional notes:_____

_____

_____

_____

Next Lesson:_____

Date: _____

Lesson start time:_____ End time:_____

Client name:_____

Dog name:_____

Phone number :_____

Additional information about the client or dog to remember?_____

_____

Does the dog have any health issues or food allergies? (Y) (N)

Does the dog have a history of aggression? (Y) (N)

Where did you do the lesson?_____

Which lesson is this?_____

What did you work on during this lesson?_____

_____

_____

Homework given to your client:_____

_____

_____

_____

Additional notes:_____

_____

_____

_____

Next Lesson:_____

Date: _____

Lesson start time:_____ End time:_____

Client name:_____

Dog name:_____

Phone number :_____

Additional information about the client or dog to remember?_____

_____

Does the dog have any health issues or food allergies? (Y) (N)

Does the dog have a history of aggression? (Y) (N)

Where did you do the lesson?_____

Which lesson is this?_____

What did you work on during this lesson?_____

_____

_____

Homework given to your client:_____

_____

_____

_____

Additional notes:_____

_____

_____

_____

Next Lesson:_____

Date: _____

Lesson start time:_____ End time:_____

Client name:_____

Dog name:_____

Phone number :_____

Additional information about the client or dog to remember?_____

_____

Does the dog have any health issues or food allergies? (Y) (N)

Does the dog have a history of aggression? (Y) (N)

Where did you do the lesson?_____

Which lesson is this?_____

What did you work on during this lesson?_____

_____

_____

Homework given to your client:_____

_____

_____

_____

Additional notes:_____

_____

_____

_____

Next Lesson:_____

Date: _____

Lesson start time:_____ End time:_____

Client name:_____

Dog name:_____

Phone number :_____

Additional information about the client or dog to remember?_____

_____

Does the dog have any health issues or food allergies? (Y) (N)

Does the dog have a history of aggression? (Y) (N)

Where did you do the lesson?_____

Which lesson is this?_____

What did you work on during this lesson?_____

_____

_____

Homework given to your client:_____

_____

_____

_____

Additional notes:_____

_____

_____

_____

Next Lesson:_____

Date: _____

Lesson start time:_____ End time:_____

Client name:_____

Dog name:_____

Phone number :_____

Additional information about the client or dog to remember?_____

_____

Does the dog have any health issues or food allergies? (Y) (N)

Does the dog have a history of aggression? (Y) (N)

Where did you do the lesson?_____

Which lesson is this?_____

What did you work on during this lesson?_____

_____

_____

Homework given to your client:_____

_____

_____

_____

Additional notes:_____

_____

_____

_____

Next Lesson:_____

Date: _____

Lesson start time:_____ End time:_____

Client name:_____

Dog name:_____

Phone number :_____

Additional information about the client or dog to remember?_____

_____

Does the dog have any health issues or food allergies? (Y) (N)

Does the dog have a history of aggression? (Y) (N)

Where did you do the lesson?_____

Which lesson is this?_____

What did you work on during this lesson?_____

_____

_____

Homework given to your client:_____

_____

_____

_____

Additional notes:_____

_____

_____

_____

Next Lesson:_____

Date: _____

Lesson start time:_____ End time:_____

Client name:_____

Dog name:_____

Phone number :_____

Additional information about the client or dog to remember?_____

_____

Does the dog have any health issues or food allergies? (Y) (N)

Does the dog have a history of aggression? (Y) (N)

Where did you do the lesson?_____

Which lesson is this?_____

What did you work on during this lesson?_____

_____

_____

Homework given to your client:_____

_____

_____

_____

Additional notes:_____

_____

_____

_____

Next Lesson:_____

Date: _____

Lesson start time:_____ End time:_____

Client name:_____

Dog name:_____

Phone number :_____

Additional information about the client or dog to remember?_____

_____

Does the dog have any health issues or food allergies? (Y) (N)

Does the dog have a history of aggression? (Y) (N)

Where did you do the lesson?_____

Which lesson is this?_____

What did you work on during this lesson?_____

_____

_____

Homework given to your client:_____

_____

_____

_____

Additional notes:_____

_____

_____

_____

Next Lesson:_____

Date: _____

Lesson start time:_____ End time:_____

Client name:_____

Dog name:_____

Phone number :_____

Additional information about the client or dog to remember?_____

_____

Does the dog have any health issues or food allergies? (Y) (N)

Does the dog have a history of aggression? (Y) (N)

Where did you do the lesson?_____

Which lesson is this?_____

What did you work on during this lesson?_____

_____

_____

Homework given to your client:_____

_____

_____

_____

Additional notes:_____

_____

_____

_____

Next Lesson:_____

Date: _____

Lesson start time:_____ End time:_____

Client name:_____

Dog name:_____

Phone number :_____

Additional information about the client or dog to remember?_____

_____

Does the dog have any health issues or food allergies? (Y) (N)

Does the dog have a history of aggression? (Y) (N)

Where did you do the lesson?_____

Which lesson is this?_____

What did you work on during this lesson?_____

_____

_____

Homework given to your client:_____

_____

_____

Additional notes:_____

_____

_____

_____

Next Lesson:_____

Date: _____

Lesson start time:_____ End time:_____

Client name:_____

Dog name:_____

Phone number :_____

Additional information about the client or dog to remember?_____

_____

Does the dog have any health issues or food allergies? (Y) (N)

Does the dog have a history of aggression? (Y) (N)

Where did you do the lesson?_____

Which lesson is this?_____

What did you work on during this lesson?_____

_____

_____

Homework given to your client:_____

_____

_____

_____

Additional notes:_____

_____

_____

_____

Next Lesson:_____

Date: _____

Lesson start time:_____ End time:_____

Client name:_____

Dog name:_____

Phone number :_____

Additional information about the client or dog to remember?_____

_____

Does the dog have any health issues or food allergies? (Y) (N)

Does the dog have a history of aggression? (Y) (N)

Where did you do the lesson?_____

Which lesson is this?_____

What did you work on during this lesson?_____

_____

_____

Homework given to your client:_____

_____

_____

_____

Additional notes:_____

_____

_____

_____

Next Lesson:_____

Date: _____

Lesson start time:_____ End time:_____

Client name:_____

Dog name:_____

Phone number :_____

Additional information about the client or dog to remember?_____

_____

Does the dog have any health issues or food allergies? (Y) (N)

Does the dog have a history of aggression? (Y) (N)

Where did you do the lesson?_____

Which lesson is this?_____

What did you work on during this lesson?_____

_____

_____

Homework given to your client:_____

_____

_____

_____

Additional notes:_____

_____

_____

_____

Next Lesson:_____

Date: _____

Lesson start time:_____ End time:_____

Client name:_____

Dog name:_____

Phone number :_____

Additional information about the client or dog to remember?_____

_____

Does the dog have any health issues or food allergies? (Y) (N)

Does the dog have a history of aggression? (Y) (N)

Where did you do the lesson?_____

Which lesson is this?_____

What did you work on during this lesson?_____

_____

_____

Homework given to your client:_____

_____

_____

_____

Additional notes:_____

_____

_____

_____

Next Lesson:_____

Date: _____

Lesson start time:_____ End time:_____

Client name:_____

Dog name:_____

Phone number :_____

Additional information about the client or dog to remember?_____

_____

Does the dog have any health issues or food allergies? (Y) (N)

Does the dog have a history of aggression? (Y) (N)

Where did you do the lesson?_____

Which lesson is this?_____

What did you work on during this lesson?_____

_____

_____

Homework given to your client:_____

_____

_____

_____

Additional notes:_____

_____

_____

_____

Next Lesson:_____

Date: _____

Lesson start time:_____ End time:_____

Client name:_____

Dog name:_____

Phone number :_____

Additional information about the client or dog to remember?_____

_____

Does the dog have any health issues or food allergies? (Y) (N)

Does the dog have a history of aggression? (Y) (N)

Where did you do the lesson?_____

Which lesson is this?_____

What did you work on during this lesson?_____

_____

_____

Homework given to your client:_____

_____

_____

_____

Additional notes:_____

_____

_____

_____

Next Lesson:_____

Date: _____

Lesson start time:_____ End time:_____

Client name:_____

Dog name:_____

Phone number :_____

Additional information about the client or dog to remember?_____

_____

Does the dog have any health issues or food allergies? (Y) (N)

Does the dog have a history of aggression? (Y) (N)

Where did you do the lesson?_____

Which lesson is this?_____

What did you work on during this lesson?_____

_____

_____

Homework given to your client:_____

_____

_____

_____

Additional notes:_____

_____

_____

_____

Next Lesson:_____

Date: _____

Lesson start time:_____ End time:_____

Client name:_____

Dog name:_____

Phone number :_____

Additional information about the client or dog to remember?_____

_____

Does the dog have any health issues or food allergies? (Y) (N)

Does the dog have a history of aggression? (Y) (N)

Where did you do the lesson?_____

Which lesson is this?_____

What did you work on during this lesson?_____

_____

_____

Homework given to your client:_____

_____

_____

_____

Additional notes:_____

_____

_____

_____

Next Lesson:_____

Date: _____

Lesson start time:_____ End time:_____

Client name:_____

Dog name:_____

Phone number :_____

Additional information about the client or dog to remember?_____

_____

Does the dog have any health issues or food allergies? (Y) (N)

Does the dog have a history of aggression? (Y) (N)

Where did you do the lesson?_____

Which lesson is this?_____

What did you work on during this lesson?_____

_____

_____

Homework given to your client:_____

_____

_____

_____

Additional notes:_____

_____

_____

_____

Next Lesson:_____

Date: _____

Lesson start time:_____ End time:_____

Client name:_____

Dog name:_____

Phone number :_____

Additional information about the client or dog to remember?_____

_____

Does the dog have any health issues or food allergies? (Y) (N)

Does the dog have a history of aggression? (Y) (N)

Where did you do the lesson?_____

Which lesson is this?_____

What did you work on during this lesson?_____

_____

_____

Homework given to your client:_____

_____

_____

_____

Additional notes:_____

_____

_____

_____

Next Lesson:_____

Date: _____

Lesson start time:_____ End time:_____

Client name:_____

Dog name:_____

Phone number :_____

Additional information about the client or dog to remember?_____

_____

Does the dog have any health issues or food allergies? (Y) (N)

Does the dog have a history of aggression? (Y) (N)

Where did you do the lesson?_____

Which lesson is this?_____

What did you work on during this lesson?_____

_____

_____

Homework given to your client:_____

_____

_____

_____

Additional notes:_____

_____

_____

_____

Next Lesson:_____

Date: _____

Lesson start time:_____ End time:_____

Client name:_____

Dog name:_____

Phone number :_____

Additional information about the client or dog to remember?_____

_____

Does the dog have any health issues or food allergies? (Y) (N)

Does the dog have a history of aggression? (Y) (N)

Where did you do the lesson?_____

Which lesson is this?_____

What did you work on during this lesson?_____

_____

_____

Homework given to your client:_____

_____

_____

_____

Additional notes:_____

_____

_____

_____

Next Lesson:_____

Date: _____

Lesson start time:_____ End time:_____

Client name:_____

Dog name:_____

Phone number :_____

Additional information about the client or dog to remember?_____

_____

Does the dog have any health issues or food allergies? (Y) (N)

Does the dog have a history of aggression? (Y) (N)

Where did you do the lesson?_____

Which lesson is this?_____

What did you work on during this lesson?_____

_____

_____

Homework given to your client:_____

_____

_____

_____

Additional notes:_____

_____

_____

_____

Next Lesson:_____

Date: _____

Lesson start time:_____ End time:_____

Client name:_____

Dog name:_____

Phone number :_____

Additional information about the client or dog to remember?_____

_____

Does the dog have any health issues or food allergies? (Y) (N)

Does the dog have a history of aggression? (Y) (N)

Where did you do the lesson?_____

Which lesson is this?_____

What did you work on during this lesson?_____

_____

_____

Homework given to your client:_____

_____

_____

_____

Additional notes:_____

_____

_____

_____

Next Lesson:_____

Date: _____

Lesson start time:_____ End time:_____

Client name:_____

Dog name:_____

Phone number :_____

Additional information about the client or dog to remember?_____

_____

Does the dog have any health issues or food allergies? (Y) (N)

Does the dog have a history of aggression? (Y) (N)

Where did you do the lesson?_____

Which lesson is this?_____

What did you work on during this lesson?_____

_____

_____

Homework given to your client:_____

_____

_____

_____

Additional notes:_____

_____

_____

_____

Next Lesson:_____

Date: _____

Lesson start time:_____ End time:_____

Client name:_____

Dog name:_____

Phone number :_____

Additional information about the client or dog to remember?_____

_____

Does the dog have any health issues or food allergies? (Y) (N)

Does the dog have a history of aggression? (Y) (N)

Where did you do the lesson?_____

Which lesson is this?_____

What did you work on during this lesson?_____

_____

_____

Homework given to your client:_____

_____

_____

_____

Additional notes:_____

_____

_____

_____

Next Lesson:_____

Date: _____

Lesson start time:_____ End time:_____

Client name:_____

Dog name:_____

Phone number :_____

Additional information about the client or dog to remember?_____

_____

Does the dog have any health issues or food allergies? (Y) (N)

Does the dog have a history of aggression? (Y) (N)

Where did you do the lesson?_____

Which lesson is this?_____

What did you work on during this lesson?_____

_____

_____

Homework given to your client:_____

_____

_____

_____

Additional notes:_____

_____

_____

_____

Next Lesson:_____

Date: _____

Lesson start time:_____ End time:_____

Client name:_____

Dog name:_____

Phone number :_____

Additional information about the client or dog to remember?_____

_____

Does the dog have any health issues or food allergies? (Y) (N)

Does the dog have a history of aggression? (Y) (N)

Where did you do the lesson?_____

Which lesson is this?_____

What did you work on during this lesson?_____

_____

_____

Homework given to your client:_____

_____

_____

_____

Additional notes:_____

_____

_____

_____

Next Lesson:_____

Date: _____

Lesson start time:_____ End time:_____

Client name:_____

Dog name:_____

Phone number :_____

Additional information about the client or dog to remember?_____

_____

Does the dog have any health issues or food allergies? (Y) (N)

Does the dog have a history of aggression? (Y) (N)

Where did you do the lesson?_____

Which lesson is this?_____

What did you work on during this lesson?_____

_____

_____

Homework given to your client:_____

_____

_____

_____

Additional notes:_____

_____

_____

_____

Next Lesson:_____

Date: _____

Lesson start time:_____ End time:_____

Client name:_____

Dog name:_____

Phone number :_____

Additional information about the client or dog to remember?_____

_____

Does the dog have any health issues or food allergies? (Y) (N)

Does the dog have a history of aggression? (Y) (N)

Where did you do the lesson?_____

Which lesson is this?_____

What did you work on during this lesson?_____

_____

_____

Homework given to your client:_____

_____

_____

_____

Additional notes:_____

_____

_____

_____

Next Lesson:_____

Date: _____

Lesson start time:_____ End time:_____

Client name:_____

Dog name:_____

Phone number :_____

Additional information about the client or dog to remember?_____

_____

Does the dog have any health issues or food allergies? (Y) (N)

Does the dog have a history of aggression? (Y) (N)

Where did you do the lesson?_____

Which lesson is this?_____

What did you work on during this lesson?_____

_____

_____

Homework given to your client:_____

_____

_____

_____

Additional notes:_____

_____

_____

_____

Next Lesson:_____

Date: _____

Lesson start time:_____ End time:_____

Client name:_____

Dog name:_____

Phone number :_____

Additional information about the client or dog to remember?_____

_____

Does the dog have any health issues or food allergies? (Y) (N)

Does the dog have a history of aggression? (Y) (N)

Where did you do the lesson?_____

Which lesson is this?_____

What did you work on during this lesson?_____

_____

_____

Homework given to your client:_____

_____

_____

_____

Additional notes:_____

_____

_____

_____

Next Lesson:_____

Date: _____

Lesson start time: _____ End time: _____

Client name: _____

Dog name: _____

Phone number : _____

Additional information about the client or dog to remember? _____

_____

Does the dog have any health issues or food allergies? (Y) (N)

Does the dog have a history of aggression? (Y) (N)

Where did you do the lesson? _____

Which lesson is this? _____

What did you work on during this lesson? _____

_____

_____

Homework given to your client: _____

_____

_____

_____

Additional notes: _____

_____

_____

_____

Next Lesson: _____

Date: _____

Lesson start time:_____ End time:_____

Client name:_____

Dog name:_____

Phone number :_____

Additional information about the client or dog to remember?_____

_____

Does the dog have any health issues or food allergies? (Y) (N)

Does the dog have a history of aggression? (Y) (N)

Where did you do the lesson?_____

Which lesson is this?_____

What did you work on during this lesson?_____

_____

_____

Homework given to your client:_____

_____

_____

_____

Additional notes:_____

_____

_____

_____

Next Lesson:_____

Date: _____

Lesson start time:_____ End time:_____

Client name:_____

Dog name:_____

Phone number :_____

Additional information about the client or dog to remember?_____

_____

Does the dog have any health issues or food allergies? (Y) (N)

Does the dog have a history of aggression? (Y) (N)

Where did you do the lesson?_____

Which lesson is this?_____

What did you work on during this lesson?_____

_____

_____

Homework given to your client:_____

_____

_____

_____

Additional notes:_____

_____

_____

_____

Next Lesson:_____

Date: _____

Lesson start time:_____ End time:_____

Client name:_____

Dog name:_____

Phone number :_____

Additional information about the client or dog to remember?_____

_____

Does the dog have any health issues or food allergies? (Y) (N)

Does the dog have a history of aggression? (Y) (N)

Where did you do the lesson?_____

Which lesson is this?_____

What did you work on during this lesson?_____

_____

_____

Homework given to your client:_____

_____

_____

_____

Additional notes:_____

_____

_____

_____

Next Lesson:_____

Date: _____

Lesson start time:_____ End time:_____

Client name:_____

Dog name:_____

Phone number :_____

Additional information about the client or dog to remember?_____

_____

Does the dog have any health issues or food allergies? (Y) (N)

Does the dog have a history of aggression? (Y) (N)

Where did you do the lesson?_____

Which lesson is this?_____

What did you work on during this lesson?_____

_____

_____

Homework given to your client:_____

_____

_____

_____

Additional notes:_____

_____

_____

_____

Next Lesson:_____

Date: _____

Lesson start time:_____ End time:_____

Client name:_____

Dog name:_____

Phone number :_____

Additional information about the client or dog to remember?_____

_____

Does the dog have any health issues or food allergies? (Y) (N)

Does the dog have a history of aggression? (Y) (N)

Where did you do the lesson?_____

Which lesson is this?_____

What did you work on during this lesson?_____

_____

_____

Homework given to your client:_____

_____

_____

_____

Additional notes:_____

_____

_____

_____

Next Lesson:_____

Date: _____

Lesson start time:_____ End time:_____

Client name:_____

Dog name:_____

Phone number :_____

Additional information about the client or dog to remember?_____

_____

Does the dog have any health issues or food allergies? (Y) (N)

Does the dog have a history of aggression? (Y) (N)

Where did you do the lesson?_____

Which lesson is this?_____

What did you work on during this lesson?_____

_____

_____

Homework given to your client:_____

_____

_____

_____

Additional notes:_____

_____

_____

_____

Next Lesson:_____

Date: _____

Lesson start time:_____ End time:_____

Client name:_____

Dog name:_____

Phone number :_____

Additional information about the client or dog to remember?_____

_____

Does the dog have any health issues or food allergies? (Y) (N)

Does the dog have a history of aggression? (Y) (N)

Where did you do the lesson?_____

Which lesson is this?_____

What did you work on during this lesson?_____

_____

_____

Homework given to your client:_____

_____

_____

_____

Additional notes:_____

_____

_____

_____

Next Lesson:_____

Date: _____

Lesson start time:_____ End time:_____

Client name:_____

Dog name:_____

Phone number :_____

Additional information about the client or dog to remember?_____

_____

Does the dog have any health issues or food allergies? (Y) (N)

Does the dog have a history of aggression? (Y) (N)

Where did you do the lesson?_____

Which lesson is this?_____

What did you work on during this lesson?_____

_____

_____

Homework given to your client:_____

_____

_____

_____

Additional notes:_____

_____

_____

_____

Next Lesson:_____

Date: _____

Lesson start time:_____ End time:_____

Client name:_____

Dog name:_____

Phone number :_____

Additional information about the client or dog to remember?_____

_____

Does the dog have any health issues or food allergies? (Y) (N)

Does the dog have a history of aggression? (Y) (N)

Where did you do the lesson?_____

Which lesson is this?_____

What did you work on during this lesson?_____

_____

_____

Homework given to your client:_____

_____

_____

_____

Additional notes:_____

_____

_____

_____

Next Lesson:_____

Date: _____

Lesson start time:_____ End time:_____

Client name:_____

Dog name:_____

Phone number :_____

Additional information about the client or dog to remember?_____

_____

Does the dog have any health issues or food allergies? (Y) (N)

Does the dog have a history of aggression? (Y) (N)

Where did you do the lesson?_____

Which lesson is this?_____

What did you work on during this lesson?_____

_____

_____

Homework given to your client:_____

_____

_____

_____

Additional notes:_____

_____

_____

_____

Next Lesson:_____

Date: _____

Lesson start time:_____ End time:_____

Client name:_____

Dog name:_____

Phone number :_____

Additional information about the client or dog to remember?_____

_____

Does the dog have any health issues or food allergies? (Y) (N)

Does the dog have a history of aggression? (Y) (N)

Where did you do the lesson?_____

Which lesson is this?_____

What did you work on during this lesson?_____

_____

_____

Homework given to your client:_____

_____

_____

Additional notes:_____

_____

_____

_____

Next Lesson:_____

Date: _____

Lesson start time:_____ End time:_____

Client name:_____

Dog name:_____

Phone number :_____

Additional information about the client or dog to remember?_____

_____

Does the dog have any health issues or food allergies? (Y) (N)

Does the dog have a history of aggression? (Y) (N)

Where did you do the lesson?_____

Which lesson is this?_____

What did you work on during this lesson?_____

_____

_____

Homework given to your client:_____

_____

_____

_____

Additional notes:_____

_____

_____

_____

Next Lesson:_____

Date: _____

Lesson start time:_____ End time:_____

Client name:_____

Dog name:_____

Phone number :_____

Additional information about the client or dog to remember?_____

_____

Does the dog have any health issues or food allergies? (Y) (N)

Does the dog have a history of aggression? (Y) (N)

Where did you do the lesson?_____

Which lesson is this?_____

What did you work on during this lesson?_____

_____

_____

Homework given to your client:_____

_____

_____

_____

Additional notes:_____

_____

_____

_____

Next Lesson:_____

Date: _____

Lesson start time:_____ End time:_____

Client name:_____

Dog name:_____

Phone number :_____

Additional information about the client or dog to remember?_____

_____

Does the dog have any health issues or food allergies? (Y) (N)

Does the dog have a history of aggression? (Y) (N)

Where did you do the lesson?_____

Which lesson is this?_____

What did you work on during this lesson?_____

_____

_____

Homework given to your client:_____

_____

_____

_____

Additional notes:_____

_____

_____

_____

Next Lesson:_____

Date: _____

Lesson start time:_____ End time:_____

Client name:_____

Dog name:_____

Phone number :_____

Additional information about the client or dog to remember?_____

_____

Does the dog have any health issues or food allergies? (Y) (N)

Does the dog have a history of aggression? (Y) (N)

Where did you do the lesson?_____

Which lesson is this?_____

What did you work on during this lesson?_____

_____

_____

Homework given to your client:_____

_____

_____

_____

Additional notes:_____

_____

_____

_____

Next Lesson:_____

Date: _____

Lesson start time:_____ End time:_____

Client name:_____

Dog name:_____

Phone number :_____

Additional information about the client or dog to remember?_____

_____

Does the dog have any health issues or food allergies? (Y) (N)

Does the dog have a history of aggression? (Y) (N)

Where did you do the lesson?_____

Which lesson is this?_____

What did you work on during this lesson?_____

_____

_____

Homework given to your client:_____

_____

_____

_____

Additional notes:_____

_____

_____

_____

Next Lesson:_____

Date: _____

Lesson start time:_____ End time:_____

Client name:_____

Dog name:_____

Phone number :_____

Additional information about the client or dog to remember?_____

_____

Does the dog have any health issues or food allergies? (Y) (N)

Does the dog have a history of aggression? (Y) (N)

Where did you do the lesson?_____

Which lesson is this?_____

What did you work on during this lesson?_____

_____

_____

Homework given to your client:_____

_____

_____

_____

Additional notes:_____

_____

_____

_____

Next Lesson:_____

Date: _____

Lesson start time:_____ End time:_____

Client name:_____

Dog name:_____

Phone number :_____

Additional information about the client or dog to remember?_____

_____

Does the dog have any health issues or food allergies? (Y) (N)

Does the dog have a history of aggression? (Y) (N)

Where did you do the lesson?_____

Which lesson is this?_____

What did you work on during this lesson?_____

_____

_____

Homework given to your client:_____

_____

_____

_____

Additional notes:_____

_____

_____

_____

Next Lesson:_____

Date: _____

Lesson start time:_____ End time:_____

Client name:_____

Dog name:_____

Phone number :_____

Additional information about the client or dog to remember?_____

_____

Does the dog have any health issues or food allergies? (Y) (N)

Does the dog have a history of aggression? (Y) (N)

Where did you do the lesson?_____

Which lesson is this?_____

What did you work on during this lesson?_____

_____

_____

Homework given to your client:_____

_____

_____

_____

Additional notes:_____

_____

_____

_____

Next Lesson:_____

Date: _____

Lesson start time:_____ End time:_____

Client name:_____

Dog name:_____

Phone number :_____

Additional information about the client or dog to remember?_____

_____

Does the dog have any health issues or food allergies? (Y) (N)

Does the dog have a history of aggression? (Y) (N)

Where did you do the lesson?_____

Which lesson is this?_____

What did you work on during this lesson?_____

_____

_____

Homework given to your client:_____

_____

_____

_____

Additional notes:_____

_____

_____

_____

Next Lesson:_____

Date: _____

Lesson start time:_____ End time:_____

Client name:_____

Dog name:_____

Phone number :_____

Additional information about the client or dog to remember?_____

_____

Does the dog have any health issues or food allergies? (Y) (N)

Does the dog have a history of aggression? (Y) (N)

Where did you do the lesson?_____

Which lesson is this?_____

What did you work on during this lesson?_____

_____

_____

Homework given to your client:_____

_____

_____

_____

Additional notes:_____

_____

_____

_____

Next Lesson:_____

Date: _____

Lesson start time:_____ End time:_____

Client name:_____

Dog name:_____

Phone number :_____

Additional information about the client or dog to remember?_____

_____

Does the dog have any health issues or food allergies? (Y) (N)

Does the dog have a history of aggression? (Y) (N)

Where did you do the lesson?_____

Which lesson is this?_____

What did you work on during this lesson?_____

_____

_____

Homework given to your client:_____

_____

_____

_____

Additional notes:_____

_____

_____

_____

Next Lesson:_____

Date: _____

Lesson start time:_____ End time:_____

Client name:_____

Dog name:_____

Phone number :_____

Additional information about the client or dog to remember?_____

_____

Does the dog have any health issues or food allergies? (Y) (N)

Does the dog have a history of aggression? (Y) (N)

Where did you do the lesson?_____

Which lesson is this?_____

What did you work on during this lesson?_____

_____

_____

Homework given to your client:_____

_____

_____

_____

Additional notes:_____

_____

_____

_____

Next Lesson:_____

Date: _____

Lesson start time:_____ End time:_____

Client name:_____

Dog name:_____

Phone number :_____

Additional information about the client or dog to remember?_____

_____

Does the dog have any health issues or food allergies? (Y) (N)

Does the dog have a history of aggression? (Y) (N)

Where did you do the lesson?_____

Which lesson is this?_____

What did you work on during this lesson?_____

_____

_____

Homework given to your client:_____

_____

_____

_____

Additional notes:_____

_____

_____

_____

Next Lesson:_____

Date: _____

Lesson start time:_____ End time:_____

Client name:_____

Dog name:_____

Phone number :_____

Additional information about the client or dog to remember?_____

_____

Does the dog have any health issues or food allergies? (Y) (N)

Does the dog have a history of aggression? (Y) (N)

Where did you do the lesson?_____

Which lesson is this?_____

What did you work on during this lesson?_____

_____

_____

Homework given to your client:_____

_____

_____

_____

Additional notes:_____

_____

_____

_____

Next Lesson:_____

Date: _____

Lesson start time:_____ End time:_____

Client name:_____

Dog name:_____

Phone number :_____

Additional information about the client or dog to remember?_____

_____

Does the dog have any health issues or food allergies? (Y) (N)

Does the dog have a history of aggression? (Y) (N)

Where did you do the lesson?_____

Which lesson is this?_____

What did you work on during this lesson?_____

_____

_____

Homework given to your client:_____

_____

_____

_____

Additional notes:_____

_____

_____

_____

Next Lesson:_____

Date: _____

Lesson start time:_____ End time:_____

Client name:_____

Dog name:_____

Phone number :_____

Additional information about the client or dog to remember?_____

_____

Does the dog have any health issues or food allergies? (Y) (N)

Does the dog have a history of aggression? (Y) (N)

Where did you do the lesson?_____

Which lesson is this?_____

What did you work on during this lesson?_____

_____

_____

Homework given to your client:_____

_____

_____

_____

Additional notes:_____

_____

_____

_____

Next Lesson:_____

Date: _____

Lesson start time:_____ End time:_____

Client name:_____

Dog name:_____

Phone number :_____

Additional information about the client or dog to remember?_____

_____

Does the dog have any health issues or food allergies? (Y) (N)

Does the dog have a history of aggression? (Y) (N)

Where did you do the lesson?_____

Which lesson is this?_____

What did you work on during this lesson?_____

_____

_____

Homework given to your client:_____

_____

_____

_____

Additional notes:_____

_____

_____

_____

Next Lesson:_____

Date: _____

Lesson start time:_____ End time:_____

Client name:_____

Dog name:_____

Phone number :_____

Additional information about the client or dog to remember?_____

_____

Does the dog have any health issues or food allergies? (Y) (N)

Does the dog have a history of aggression? (Y) (N)

Where did you do the lesson?_____

Which lesson is this?_____

What did you work on during this lesson?_____

_____

_____

Homework given to your client:_____

_____

_____

_____

Additional notes:_____

_____

_____

_____

Next Lesson:_____

Date: _____

Lesson start time:_____ End time:_____

Client name:_____

Dog name:_____

Phone number :_____

Additional information about the client or dog to remember?_____

_____

Does the dog have any health issues or food allergies? (Y) (N)

Does the dog have a history of aggression? (Y) (N)

Where did you do the lesson?_____

Which lesson is this?_____

What did you work on during this lesson?_____

_____

_____

Homework given to your client:_____

_____

_____

_____

Additional notes:_____

_____

_____

_____

Next Lesson:_____

Date: _____

Lesson start time:_____ End time:_____

Client name:_____

Dog name:_____

Phone number :_____

Additional information about the client or dog to remember?_____

_____

Does the dog have any health issues or food allergies? (Y) (N)

Does the dog have a history of aggression? (Y) (N)

Where did you do the lesson?_____

Which lesson is this?_____

What did you work on during this lesson?_____

_____

_____

Homework given to your client:_____

_____

_____

_____

Additional notes:_____

_____

_____

_____

Next Lesson:_____

Date: _____

Lesson start time:_____ End time:_____

Client name:_____

Dog name:_____

Phone number :_____

Additional information about the client or dog to remember?_____

_____

Does the dog have any health issues or food allergies? (Y) (N)

Does the dog have a history of aggression? (Y) (N)

Where did you do the lesson?_____

Which lesson is this?_____

What did you work on during this lesson?_____

_____

_____

Homework given to your client:_____

_____

_____

_____

Additional notes:_____

_____

_____

_____

Next Lesson:_____

Date: _____

Lesson start time:_____ End time:_____

Client name:_____

Dog name:_____

Phone number :_____

Additional information about the client or dog to remember?_____

_____

Does the dog have any health issues or food allergies? (Y) (N)

Does the dog have a history of aggression? (Y) (N)

Where did you do the lesson?_____

Which lesson is this?_____

What did you work on during this lesson?_____

_____

_____

Homework given to your client:_____

_____

_____

_____

Additional notes:_____

_____

_____

_____

Next Lesson:_____

Date: _____

Lesson start time:_____ End time:_____

Client name:_____

Dog name:_____

Phone number :_____

Additional information about the client or dog to remember?_____

_____

Does the dog have any health issues or food allergies? (Y) (N)

Does the dog have a history of aggression? (Y) (N)

Where did you do the lesson?_____

Which lesson is this?_____

What did you work on during this lesson?_____

_____

_____

Homework given to your client:_____

_____

_____

_____

Additional notes:_____

_____

_____

_____

Next Lesson:_____

Date: _____

Lesson start time:_____ End time:_____

Client name:_____

Dog name:_____

Phone number :_____

Additional information about the client or dog to remember?_____

_____

Does the dog have any health issues or food allergies? (Y) (N)

Does the dog have a history of aggression? (Y) (N)

Where did you do the lesson?_____

Which lesson is this?_____

What did you work on during this lesson?_____

_____

_____

Homework given to your client:_____

_____

_____

_____

Additional notes:_____

_____

_____

_____

Next Lesson:_____

Date: _____

Lesson start time:_____ End time:_____

Client name:_____

Dog name:_____

Phone number :_____

Additional information about the client or dog to remember?_____

_____

Does the dog have any health issues or food allergies? (Y) (N)

Does the dog have a history of aggression? (Y) (N)

Where did you do the lesson?_____

Which lesson is this?_____

What did you work on during this lesson?_____

_____

_____

Homework given to your client:_____

_____

_____

_____

Additional notes:_____

_____

_____

_____

Next Lesson:_____

Date: _____

Lesson start time:_____ End time:_____

Client name:_____

Dog name:_____

Phone number :_____

Additional information about the client or dog to remember?_____

_____

Does the dog have any health issues or food allergies? (Y) (N)

Does the dog have a history of aggression? (Y) (N)

Where did you do the lesson?_____

Which lesson is this?_____

What did you work on during this lesson?_____

_____

_____

Homework given to your client:_____

_____

_____

_____

Additional notes:_____

_____

_____

_____

Next Lesson:_____

Date: _____

Lesson start time:_____ End time:_____

Client name:_____

Dog name:_____

Phone number :_____

Additional information about the client or dog to remember?_____

_____

Does the dog have any health issues or food allergies? (Y) (N)

Does the dog have a history of aggression? (Y) (N)

Where did you do the lesson?_____

Which lesson is this?_____

What did you work on during this lesson?_____

_____

_____

Homework given to your client:_____

_____

_____

_____

Additional notes:_____

_____

_____

_____

Next Lesson:_____

Date: _____

Lesson start time:_____ End time:_____

Client name:_____

Dog name:_____

Phone number :_____

Additional information about the client or dog to remember?_____

_____

Does the dog have any health issues or food allergies? (Y) (N)

Does the dog have a history of aggression? (Y) (N)

Where did you do the lesson?_____

Which lesson is this?_____

What did you work on during this lesson?_____

_____

_____

Homework given to your client:_____

_____

_____

_____

Additional notes:_____

_____

_____

_____

Next Lesson:_____

Date: _____

Lesson start time:_____ End time:_____

Client name:_____

Dog name:_____

Phone number :_____

Additional information about the client or dog to remember?_____

_____

Does the dog have any health issues or food allergies? (Y) (N)

Does the dog have a history of aggression? (Y) (N)

Where did you do the lesson?_____

Which lesson is this?_____

What did you work on during this lesson?_____

_____

_____

Homework given to your client:_____

_____

_____

_____

Additional notes:_____

_____

_____

_____

Next Lesson:_____

Date: _____

Lesson start time:_____ End time:_____

Client name:_____

Dog name:_____

Phone number :_____

Additional information about the client or dog to remember?_____

_____

Does the dog have any health issues or food allergies? (Y) (N)

Does the dog have a history of aggression? (Y) (N)

Where did you do the lesson?_____

Which lesson is this?_____

What did you work on during this lesson?_____

_____

_____

Homework given to your client:_____

_____

_____

_____

Additional notes:_____

_____

_____

_____

Next Lesson:_____

Date: _____

Lesson start time:_____ End time:_____

Client name:_____

Dog name:_____

Phone number :_____

Additional information about the client or dog to remember?_____

_____

Does the dog have any health issues or food allergies? (Y) (N)

Does the dog have a history of aggression? (Y) (N)

Where did you do the lesson?_____

Which lesson is this?_____

What did you work on during this lesson?_____

_____

_____

Homework given to your client:_____

_____

_____

_____

Additional notes:_____

_____

_____

_____

Next Lesson:_____

Date: _____

Lesson start time:_____ End time:_____

Client name:_____

Dog name:_____

Phone number :_____

Additional information about the client or dog to remember?_____

_____

Does the dog have any health issues or food allergies? (Y) (N)

Does the dog have a history of aggression? (Y) (N)

Where did you do the lesson?_____

Which lesson is this?_____

What did you work on during this lesson?_____

_____

_____

Homework given to your client:_____

_____

_____

_____

Additional notes:_____

_____

_____

_____

Next Lesson:_____

Date: _____

Lesson start time:_____ End time:_____

Client name:_____

Dog name:_____

Phone number :_____

Additional information about the client or dog to remember?_____

_____

Does the dog have any health issues or food allergies? (Y) (N)

Does the dog have a history of aggression? (Y) (N)

Where did you do the lesson?_____

Which lesson is this?_____

What did you work on during this lesson?_____

_____

_____

Homework given to your client:_____

_____

_____

_____

Additional notes:_____

_____

_____

_____

Next Lesson:_____

Date: _____

Lesson start time:_____ End time:_____

Client name:_____

Dog name:_____

Phone number :_____

Additional information about the client or dog to remember?_____

_____

Does the dog have any health issues or food allergies? (Y) (N)

Does the dog have a history of aggression? (Y) (N)

Where did you do the lesson?_____

Which lesson is this?_____

What did you work on during this lesson?_____

_____

_____

Homework given to your client:_____

_____

_____

_____

Additional notes:_____

_____

_____

_____

Next Lesson:_____

Date: _____

Lesson start time:_____ End time:_____

Client name:_____

Dog name:_____

Phone number :_____

Additional information about the client or dog to remember?_____

_____

Does the dog have any health issues or food allergies? (Y) (N)

Does the dog have a history of aggression? (Y) (N)

Where did you do the lesson?_____

Which lesson is this?_____

What did you work on during this lesson?_____

_____

_____

Homework given to your client:_____

_____

_____

_____

Additional notes:_____

_____

_____

_____

Next Lesson:_____

Date: _____

Lesson start time:_____ End time:_____

Client name:_____

Dog name:_____

Phone number :_____

Additional information about the client or dog to remember?_____

_____

Does the dog have any health issues or food allergies? (Y) (N)

Does the dog have a history of aggression? (Y) (N)

Where did you do the lesson?_____

Which lesson is this?_____

What did you work on during this lesson?_____

_____

_____

Homework given to your client:_____

_____

_____

_____

Additional notes:_____

_____

_____

_____

Next Lesson:_____

Date: _____

Lesson start time:_____ End time:_____

Client name:_____

Dog name:_____

Phone number :_____

Additional information about the client or dog to remember?_____

_____

Does the dog have any health issues or food allergies? (Y) (N)

Does the dog have a history of aggression? (Y) (N)

Where did you do the lesson?_____

Which lesson is this?_____

What did you work on during this lesson?_____

_____

_____

Homework given to your client:_____

_____

_____

_____

Additional notes:_____

_____

_____

_____

Next Lesson:_____

Date: _____

Lesson start time:_____ End time:_____

Client name:_____

Dog name:_____

Phone number :_____

Additional information about the client or dog to remember?_____

_____

Does the dog have any health issues or food allergies? (Y) (N)

Does the dog have a history of aggression? (Y) (N)

Where did you do the lesson?_____

Which lesson is this?_____

What did you work on during this lesson?_____

_____

_____

Homework given to your client:_____

_____

_____

_____

Additional notes:_____

_____

_____

_____

Next Lesson:_____

Date: _____

Lesson start time:_____ End time:_____

Client name:_____

Dog name:_____

Phone number :_____

Additional information about the client or dog to remember?_____

_____

Does the dog have any health issues or food allergies? (Y) (N)

Does the dog have a history of aggression? (Y) (N)

Where did you do the lesson?_____

Which lesson is this?_____

What did you work on during this lesson?_____

_____

_____

Homework given to your client:_____

_____

_____

_____

Additional notes:_____

_____

_____

_____

Next Lesson:_____

Date: _____

Lesson start time:_____ End time:_____

Client name:_____

Dog name:_____

Phone number :_____

Additional information about the client or dog to remember?_____

_____

Does the dog have any health issues or food allergies? (Y) (N)

Does the dog have a history of aggression? (Y) (N)

Where did you do the lesson?_____

Which lesson is this?_____

What did you work on during this lesson?_____

_____

_____

Homework given to your client:_____

_____

_____

_____

Additional notes:_____

_____

_____

_____

Next Lesson:_____

Date: _____

Lesson start time:_____ End time:_____

Client name:_____

Dog name:_____

Phone number :_____

Additional information about the client or dog to remember?_____

_____

Does the dog have any health issues or food allergies? (Y) (N)

Does the dog have a history of aggression? (Y) (N)

Where did you do the lesson?_____

Which lesson is this?_____

What did you work on during this lesson?_____

_____

_____

Homework given to your client:_____

_____

_____

_____

Additional notes:_____

_____

_____

_____

Next Lesson:_____

Date: _____

Lesson start time:_____ End time:_____

Client name:_____

Dog name:_____

Phone number :_____

Additional information about the client or dog to remember?_____

_____

Does the dog have any health issues or food allergies? (Y) (N)

Does the dog have a history of aggression? (Y) (N)

Where did you do the lesson?_____

Which lesson is this?_____

What did you work on during this lesson?_____

_____

_____

Homework given to your client:_____

_____

_____

_____

Additional notes:_____

_____

_____

_____

Next Lesson:_____

Date: _____

Lesson start time:_____ End time:_____

Client name:_____

Dog name:_____

Phone number :_____

Additional information about the client or dog to remember?_____

_____

Does the dog have any health issues or food allergies? (Y) (N)

Does the dog have a history of aggression? (Y) (N)

Where did you do the lesson?_____

Which lesson is this?_____

What did you work on during this lesson?_____

_____

_____

Homework given to your client:_____

_____

_____

_____

Additional notes:_____

_____

_____

_____

Next Lesson:_____

Date: _____

Lesson start time:_____ End time:_____

Client name:_____

Dog name:_____

Phone number :_____

Additional information about the client or dog to remember?_____

_____

Does the dog have any health issues or food allergies? (Y) (N)

Does the dog have a history of aggression? (Y) (N)

Where did you do the lesson?_____

Which lesson is this?_____

What did you work on during this lesson?_____

_____

_____

Homework given to your client:_____

_____

_____

_____

Additional notes:_____

_____

_____

_____

Next Lesson:_____

Date: _____

Lesson start time:_____ End time:_____

Client name:_____

Dog name:_____

Phone number :_____

Additional information about the client or dog to remember?_____

_____

Does the dog have any health issues or food allergies? (Y) (N)

Does the dog have a history of aggression? (Y) (N)

Where did you do the lesson?_____

Which lesson is this?_____

What did you work on during this lesson?_____

_____

_____

Homework given to your client:_____

_____

_____

_____

Additional notes:_____

_____

_____

_____

Next Lesson:_____

Date: _____

Lesson start time:_____ End time:_____

Client name:_____

Dog name:_____

Phone number :_____

Additional information about the client or dog to remember?_____

_____

Does the dog have any health issues or food allergies? (Y) (N)

Does the dog have a history of aggression? (Y) (N)

Where did you do the lesson?_____

Which lesson is this?_____

What did you work on during this lesson?_____

_____

_____

Homework given to your client:_____

_____

_____

_____

Additional notes:_____

_____

_____

_____

Next Lesson:_____

Date: _____

Lesson start time:_____ End time:_____

Client name:_____

Dog name:_____

Phone number :_____

Additional information about the client or dog to remember?_____

_____

Does the dog have any health issues or food allergies? (Y) (N)

Does the dog have a history of aggression? (Y) (N)

Where did you do the lesson?_____

Which lesson is this?_____

What did you work on during this lesson?_____

_____

_____

Homework given to your client:_____

_____

_____

_____

Additional notes:_____

_____

_____

_____

Next Lesson:_____

Date: _____

Lesson start time:_____ End time:_____

Client name:_____

Dog name:_____

Phone number :_____

Additional information about the client or dog to remember?_____

_____

Does the dog have any health issues or food allergies? (Y) (N)

Does the dog have a history of aggression? (Y) (N)

Where did you do the lesson?_____

Which lesson is this?_____

What did you work on during this lesson?_____

_____

_____

Homework given to your client:_____

_____

_____

_____

Additional notes:_____

_____

_____

_____

Next Lesson:_____

Date: _____

Lesson start time:_____ End time:_____

Client name:_____

Dog name:_____

Phone number :_____

Additional information about the client or dog to remember?_____

_____

Does the dog have any health issues or food allergies? (Y) (N)

Does the dog have a history of aggression? (Y) (N)

Where did you do the lesson?_____

Which lesson is this?_____

What did you work on during this lesson?_____

_____

_____

Homework given to your client:_____

_____

_____

_____

Additional notes:_____

_____

_____

_____

Next Lesson:_____

Date: _____

Lesson start time:_____ End time:_____

Client name:_____

Dog name:_____

Phone number :_____

Additional information about the client or dog to remember?_____

_____

Does the dog have any health issues or food allergies? (Y) (N)

Does the dog have a history of aggression? (Y) (N)

Where did you do the lesson?_____

Which lesson is this?_____

What did you work on during this lesson?_____

_____

_____

Homework given to your client:_____

_____

_____

_____

Additional notes:_____

_____

_____

_____

Next Lesson:_____

Date: _____

Lesson start time:_____ End time:_____

Client name:_____

Dog name:_____

Phone number :_____

Additional information about the client or dog to remember?_____

_____

Does the dog have any health issues or food allergies? (Y) (N)

Does the dog have a history of aggression? (Y) (N)

Where did you do the lesson?_____

Which lesson is this?_____

What did you work on during this lesson?_____

_____

_____

Homework given to your client:_____

_____

_____

_____

Additional notes:_____

_____

_____

_____

Next Lesson:_____

Date: _____

Lesson start time:_____ End time:_____

Client name:_____

Dog name:_____

Phone number :_____

Additional information about the client or dog to remember?_____

_____

Does the dog have any health issues or food allergies? (Y) (N)

Does the dog have a history of aggression? (Y) (N)

Where did you do the lesson?_____

Which lesson is this?_____

What did you work on during this lesson?_____

_____

_____

Homework given to your client:_____

_____

_____

_____

Additional notes:_____

_____

_____

_____

Next Lesson:_____

Date: _____

Lesson start time:_____ End time:_____

Client name:_____

Dog name:_____

Phone number :_____

Additional information about the client or dog to remember?_____

_____

Does the dog have any health issues or food allergies? (Y) (N)

Does the dog have a history of aggression? (Y) (N)

Where did you do the lesson?_____

Which lesson is this?_____

What did you work on during this lesson?_____

_____

_____

Homework given to your client:_____

_____

_____

_____

Additional notes:_____

_____

_____

_____

Next Lesson:_____

Date: _____

Lesson start time:_____ End time:_____

Client name:_____

Dog name:_____

Phone number :_____

Additional information about the client or dog to remember?_____

_____

Does the dog have any health issues or food allergies? (Y) (N)

Does the dog have a history of aggression? (Y) (N)

Where did you do the lesson?_____

Which lesson is this?_____

What did you work on during this lesson?_____

_____

_____

Homework given to your client:_____

_____

_____

_____

Additional notes:_____

_____

_____

_____

Next Lesson:_____

Date: _____

Lesson start time:_____ End time:_____

Client name:_____

Dog name:_____

Phone number :_____

Additional information about the client or dog to remember?_____

_____

Does the dog have any health issues or food allergies? (Y) (N)

Does the dog have a history of aggression? (Y) (N)

Where did you do the lesson?_____

Which lesson is this?_____

What did you work on during this lesson?_____

_____

_____

Homework given to your client:_____

_____

_____

_____

Additional notes:_____

_____

_____

_____

Next Lesson:_____

Date: _____

Lesson start time:_____ End time:_____

Client name:_____

Dog name:_____

Phone number :_____

Additional information about the client or dog to remember?_____

_____

Does the dog have any health issues or food allergies? (Y) (N)

Does the dog have a history of aggression? (Y) (N)

Where did you do the lesson?_____

Which lesson is this?_____

What did you work on during this lesson?_____

_____

_____

Homework given to your client:_____

_____

_____

_____

Additional notes:_____

_____

_____

_____

Next Lesson:_____

Date: _____

Lesson start time:_____ End time:_____

Client name:_____

Dog name:_____

Phone number :_____

Additional information about the client or dog to remember?_____

_____

Does the dog have any health issues or food allergies? (Y) (N)

Does the dog have a history of aggression? (Y) (N)

Where did you do the lesson?_____

Which lesson is this?_____

What did you work on during this lesson?_____

_____

_____

Homework given to your client:_____

_____

_____

_____

Additional notes:_____

_____

_____

_____

Next Lesson:_____

Date: _____

Lesson start time:_____ End time:_____

Client name:_____

Dog name:_____

Phone number :_____

Additional information about the client or dog to remember?_____

_____

Does the dog have any health issues or food allergies? (Y) (N)

Does the dog have a history of aggression? (Y) (N)

Where did you do the lesson?_____

Which lesson is this?_____

What did you work on during this lesson?_____

_____

_____

Homework given to your client:_____

_____

_____

_____

Additional notes:_____

_____

_____

_____

Next Lesson:_____

Date: _____

Lesson start time:_____ End time:_____

Client name:_____

Dog name:_____

Phone number :_____

Additional information about the client or dog to remember?_____

_____

Does the dog have any health issues or food allergies? (Y) (N)

Does the dog have a history of aggression? (Y) (N)

Where did you do the lesson?_____

Which lesson is this?_____

What did you work on during this lesson?_____

_____

_____

Homework given to your client:_____

_____

_____

_____

Additional notes:_____

_____

_____

_____

Next Lesson:_____

Date: _____

Lesson start time:_____ End time:_____

Client name:_____

Dog name:_____

Phone number :_____

Additional information about the client or dog to remember?_____

_____

Does the dog have any health issues or food allergies? (Y) (N)

Does the dog have a history of aggression? (Y) (N)

Where did you do the lesson?_____

Which lesson is this?_____

What did you work on during this lesson?_____

_____

_____

Homework given to your client:_____

_____

_____

_____

Additional notes:_____

_____

_____

_____

Next Lesson:_____

Date: _____

Lesson start time:_____ End time:_____

Client name:_____

Dog name:_____

Phone number :_____

Additional information about the client or dog to remember?_____

_____

Does the dog have any health issues or food allergies? (Y) (N)

Does the dog have a history of aggression? (Y) (N)

Where did you do the lesson?_____

Which lesson is this?_____

What did you work on during this lesson?_____

_____

_____

Homework given to your client:_____

_____

_____

_____

Additional notes:_____

_____

_____

_____

Next Lesson:_____

Date: _____

Lesson start time:_____ End time:_____

Client name:_____

Dog name:_____

Phone number :_____

Additional information about the client or dog to remember?_____

_____

Does the dog have any health issues or food allergies? (Y) (N)

Does the dog have a history of aggression? (Y) (N)

Where did you do the lesson?_____

Which lesson is this?_____

What did you work on during this lesson?_____

_____

_____

Homework given to your client:_____

_____

_____

_____

Additional notes:_____

_____

_____

_____

Next Lesson:_____

Date: _____

Lesson start time:_____ End time:_____

Client name:_____

Dog name:_____

Phone number :_____

Additional information about the client or dog to remember?_____

_____

Does the dog have any health issues or food allergies? (Y) (N)

Does the dog have a history of aggression? (Y) (N)

Where did you do the lesson?_____

Which lesson is this?_____

What did you work on during this lesson?_____

_____

_____

Homework given to your client:_____

_____

_____

_____

Additional notes:_____

_____

_____

_____

Next Lesson:_____

Date: _____

Lesson start time:_____ End time:_____

Client name:_____

Dog name:_____

Phone number :_____

Additional information about the client or dog to remember?_____

_____

Does the dog have any health issues or food allergies? (Y) (N)

Does the dog have a history of aggression? (Y) (N)

Where did you do the lesson?_____

Which lesson is this?_____

What did you work on during this lesson?_____

_____

_____

Homework given to your client:_____

_____

_____

_____

Additional notes:_____

_____

_____

_____

Next Lesson:_____

Date: _____

Lesson start time:_____ End time:_____

Client name:_____

Dog name:_____

Phone number :_____

Additional information about the client or dog to remember?_____

_____

Does the dog have any health issues or food allergies? (Y) (N)

Does the dog have a history of aggression? (Y) (N)

Where did you do the lesson?_____

Which lesson is this?_____

What did you work on during this lesson?_____

_____

_____

Homework given to your client:_____

_____

_____

_____

Additional notes:_____

_____

_____

_____

Next Lesson:_____

Date: _____

Lesson start time:_____ End time:_____

Client name:_____

Dog name:_____

Phone number :_____

Additional information about the client or dog to remember?_____

_____

Does the dog have any health issues or food allergies? (Y) (N)

Does the dog have a history of aggression? (Y) (N)

Where did you do the lesson?_____

Which lesson is this?_____

What did you work on during this lesson?_____

_____

_____

Homework given to your client:_____

_____

_____

_____

Additional notes:_____

_____

_____

_____

Next Lesson:_____

Date: _____

Lesson start time:_____ End time:_____

Client name:_____

Dog name:_____

Phone number :_____

Additional information about the client or dog to remember?_____

_____

Does the dog have any health issues or food allergies? (Y) (N)

Does the dog have a history of aggression? (Y) (N)

Where did you do the lesson?_____

Which lesson is this?_____

What did you work on during this lesson?_____

_____

_____

Homework given to your client:_____

_____

_____

_____

Additional notes:_____

_____

_____

_____

Next Lesson:_____

Date: _____

Lesson start time:_____ End time:_____

Client name:_____

Dog name:_____

Phone number :_____

Additional information about the client or dog to remember?_____

_____

Does the dog have any health issues or food allergies? (Y) (N)

Does the dog have a history of aggression? (Y) (N)

Where did you do the lesson?_____

Which lesson is this?_____

What did you work on during this lesson?_____

_____

_____

Homework given to your client:_____

_____

_____

_____

Additional notes:_____

_____

_____

_____

Next Lesson:_____

Date: _____

Lesson start time:_____ End time:_____

Client name:_____

Dog name:_____

Phone number :_____

Additional information about the client or dog to remember?_____

_____

Does the dog have any health issues or food allergies? (Y) (N)

Does the dog have a history of aggression? (Y) (N)

Where did you do the lesson?_____

Which lesson is this?_____

What did you work on during this lesson?_____

_____

_____

Homework given to your client:_____

_____

_____

_____

Additional notes:_____

_____

_____

_____

Next Lesson:_____

Date: _____

Lesson start time:_____ End time:_____

Client name:_____

Dog name:_____

Phone number :_____

Additional information about the client or dog to remember?_____

_____

Does the dog have any health issues or food allergies? (Y) (N)

Does the dog have a history of aggression? (Y) (N)

Where did you do the lesson?_____

Which lesson is this?_____

What did you work on during this lesson?_____

_____

_____

Homework given to your client:_____

_____

_____

_____

Additional notes:_____

_____

_____

_____

Next Lesson:_____

Date: _____

Lesson start time:_____ End time:_____

Client name:_____

Dog name:_____

Phone number :_____

Additional information about the client or dog to remember?_____

_____

Does the dog have any health issues or food allergies? (Y) (N)

Does the dog have a history of aggression? (Y) (N)

Where did you do the lesson?_____

Which lesson is this?_____

What did you work on during this lesson?_____

_____

_____

Homework given to your client:_____

_____

_____

_____

Additional notes:_____

_____

_____

_____

Next Lesson:_____

Date: _____

Lesson start time:_____ End time:_____

Client name:_____

Dog name:_____

Phone number : _____

Additional information about the client or dog to remember?_____

_____

Does the dog have any health issues or food allergies? (Y) (N)

Does the dog have a history of aggression? (Y) (N)

Where did you do the lesson?_____

Which lesson is this?_____

What did you work on during this lesson?_____

_____

_____

Homework given to your client:_____

_____

_____

_____

Additional notes:_____

_____

_____

_____

Next Lesson:_____

Date: _____

Lesson start time:_____ End time:_____

Client name:_____

Dog name:_____

Phone number :_____

Additional information about the client or dog to remember?_____

_____

Does the dog have any health issues or food allergies? (Y) (N)

Does the dog have a history of aggression? (Y) (N)

Where did you do the lesson?_____

Which lesson is this?_____

What did you work on during this lesson?_____

_____

_____

Homework given to your client:_____

_____

_____

_____

Additional notes:_____

_____

_____

_____

Next Lesson:_____

Date: _____

Lesson start time:_____ End time:_____

Client name:_____

Dog name:_____

Phone number :_____

Additional information about the client or dog to remember?_____

_____

Does the dog have any health issues or food allergies? (Y) (N)

Does the dog have a history of aggression? (Y) (N)

Where did you do the lesson?_____

Which lesson is this?_____

What did you work on during this lesson?_____

_____

_____

Homework given to your client:_____

_____

_____

_____

Additional notes:_____

_____

_____

_____

Next Lesson:_____

Made in the USA
Monee, IL
25 September 2019